HISTORY OF FUN STUFF

The Explosive Story of Fireworks!

by Kama Einhorn
illustrated by Daniel Guidera

Ready-to-Read

Simon Spotlight

New York   London   Toronto   Sydney   New Delhi

SIMON SPOTLIGHT
An imprint of Simon & Schuster Children's Publishing Division
1230 Avenue of the Americas, New York, New York 10020
This Simon Spotlight edition June 2015
Text copyright © 2015 by Simon & Schuster, Inc.
Illustrations copyright © 2015 by Daniel Guidera

For information about special discounts for bulk purchases, please contact Simon & Schuster Special Sales at
1-866-506-1949 or business@simonandschuster.com.
Manufactured in the United States of America 0121 LAK
4 6 8 10 9 7 5 3
Library of Congress Cataloging-in-Publication Data
Einhorn, Kama, 1969–
The explosive story of fireworks! / by Kama Einhorn ; illustrated by Daniel Guidera.
pages cm. — (History of fun stuff)
Includes bibliographical references and index.
Audience: Ages 6–8.
Audience: Grades K to 3.
1. Fireworks—History—Juvenile literature. I. Guidera, Daniel, illustrator. II. Title.
TP300.E35 2015
662'.1—dc23
2014031762
ISBN 978-1-4814-3848-3 (hc)
ISBN 978-1-4814-3847-6 (pbk)
ISBN 978-1-4814-3849-0 (eBook)

CONTENTS

CHAPTER 1
The First Fireworks

Boom! Bam! Bang! You've probably oohed and aahed as you gazed up at Fourth of July fireworks bursting in the night sky over your city or town. Or maybe you've stayed up until midnight on New Year's Eve to watch the sparkly explosions wow the crowds in Times Square.

What do you think about fireworks? Most people love them, but your dog may not be a big fan of their loud noises. Perhaps you agree. Or maybe you just think fireworks are totally pretty. But do you know where these dazzling displays come from, or how people figured out how to create them? Get ready to become a History of Fun Stuff Expert on fireworks!

Let's travel way back in time to 200 BC, to the Han Dynasty of ancient China. Most historians agree that the first "fireworks" were bamboo stalks. People would roast the hollow green reeds to make them blacken, sizzle, and explode. The air inside the bamboo made a natural firecracker. *Pop!* The loud sound scared people and animals, so it was used to keep evil spirits away.

9

But bamboo alone can't make bright light. To make firecrackers actually *flash*, gunpowder was needed. That was invented hundreds of years later, between 600 and 900 AD. Early scientists in China (called alchemists) made gunpowder by combining certain ingredients with saltpeter (potassium nitrate). By filling bamboo shoots with gunpowder, they discovered that the shoots would create a big flash and boom when ignited. With a pop and a flash, the first fireworks had exploded into the world!

Firecrackers and fireworks were set off at the beginning of the Chinese New Year to scare off evil spirits. Even today, firecrackers and fireworks are still a big part of many Chinese New Year celebrations.

Before long, firecrackers were made using paper tubes rather than bamboo stalks. And then people began putting firecrackers on arrows during battle. The enemies saw lightninglike explosions coming from the sky, and were terrified!

CHAPTER 2
Fireworks Explode in Europe

Of course, fireworks didn't stay only in China forever. Some historians credit the Italian traveler Marco Polo with bringing gunpowder from the east to Europe in the thirteenth century. No matter how they traveled, fireworks soon became popular in Europe.

By the fifteenth century, fireworks had become part of European celebrations, like those for weddings or victories in war. In England "fire masters" would put on fireworks displays with the help of their assistants, called "green men."

Green men had a pretty dangerous job. Because sparks would rain down on them, they wore caps of leaves to avoid being burned. They would also entertain spectators as the fire masters got everything ready for the fireworks show.

English royalty had a fascination with fireworks. In fact, the earliest known fireworks display in England occurred in 1486, for the wedding of Henry VII.

And Henry VII's son, Henry VIII, also set off a spectacular fireworks display to celebrate his wedding to Anne Boleyn in 1533. There is a record of a fire-breathing dragon that was made using fireworks!

The daughter of Henry VIII and Anne Boleyn was Queen Elizabeth I. She was the Queen of England from 1558 to 1603. She loved fireworks so much that she even created a special title for the person who made the best fireworks show. And later, in 1685, King James II was so happy with the fireworks display at his crowning ceremony that he made his fire master a knight!

All over Europe rulers used fireworks to enchant, amaze, and delight their people, lighting up their castles on special occasions to show their wealth and power.

In the 1830s the night sky *really* began to glimmer and shimmer. Italians became famous for turning fireworks into a new art form. They invented shells—canisters that could be launched into the sky. And they added metals and chemicals to the gunpowder to make different colors. Before this, fireworks were orange and white flashes of light.

ITALY

For instance, barium makes fireworks green, sodium makes them yellow, lithium and strontium make them red, and copper makes them blue. To get a purple color, the chemicals to make red and blue fireworks are mixed together.

CHAPTER 3
Fourth of July Fireworks

So how did fireworks make it across the Atlantic Ocean to the United States? The British colonists—the first settlers—brought them along by boat.

Legend says that the first fireworks in American skies were set off by Captain John Smith in Jamestown, Virginia, in 1608, impressing (or perhaps scaring) nearby Native Americans.

On July 3, 1776, the day before the Declaration of Independence was adopted, founding father (and future president) John Adams wrote a letter to his wife, Abigail, describing a bright idea. It was to use fireworks to celebrate America's independence from England.

The next year was the very first July
Fourth celebration! The United States was
still fighting the Revolutionary War against
England, but those fireworks probably
gave these new Americans more than a
few sparks of hope.

Fireworks remained popular in the United States as the years went on. But not everyone was happy about it. In 1906 the Society for the Suppression of Unnecessary Noise was formed, which eventually

pushed for restrictions on fireworks. And that wasn't the first time fireworks were restricted. There was a law passed in Rhode Island in 1731 that banned "mischievous use of" fireworks!

Government leaders and lawmakers wanted to keep the Fourth of July tradition going, but they also wanted to make sure all fireworks displays were safe. States passed laws governing the use of fireworks and explosives. The federal government also has regulations about the kind of small fireworks people can buy and the safety labels they have to have. Fireworks are dangerous and must always be handled responsibly and by an adult.

CHAPTER 4
Lighting Up the Night

Flashy displays, of course, are still a Fourth of July tradition. Each year pyrotechnicians ("pie-row-teck-NISH-uns") try to outdo themselves and each other and wow the crowds with colorful showers of sparks. Plus, firework technology has . . . well . . . exploded!

There are new colors like salmon and aqua. And now fireworks' light can be made to look like it's squiggling and wiggling, cascading down in bright flakes, or shooting up like water from a hose. It can be made to look as if it's blasting up like a rocket, raining down tiny specks of confetti, twinkling or flashing on and off, changing color midburst, or radiating luminous pom-poms. Not bad for something that started out as stalks of green bamboo!

And remember how the Italians became famous for turning fireworks into an art form? Glimmers of that are still visible in the sky today. That's because many of the leading American companies that put on big fireworks shows are owned and operated by families of Italian descent, such as the Gruccis, Rozzis, and Zambellis.

And people keep finding ways to make fireworks shows even better. Disneyland now uses compressed air—not gunpowder—to launch fireworks. The pyrotechnicians there also started using electronic timers to explode the shells so that they burst at a certain time. This way fireworks shows can be set to music and choreographed, just like a dance.

Besides Disney, where there are fireworks every night, some huge shows can be seen on the Fourth of July in New York City, in Washington, DC, on the National Mall, and in Boston along the Charles River. What do you think the fireworks of the future will look like?

HISTORY OF FUN STUFF EXPERT ON FIREWORKS!

Congratulations! You've come to the end of this book. You are now an official History of Fun Stuff Expert on fireworks. Go ahead and impress your friends and family with all your sparkling knowledge about where those shimmers in the sky came from. And next time you look up to see fireworks, think about the years of history that went into them as you *ooh!* and *aah!*

Hey, kids! Now that you're an expert on the history of fireworks, turn the page to learn even more about fireworks and some science, world cultures, and art along the way!

All About Bamboo

Bamboo is a special plant, and not just because the ancient Chinese used it to make the first fireworks! Bamboo can grow really fast and really tall, and it's actually a member of the grass family. That's right, bamboo isn't a tree at all—it's grass! Check out these other fun facts about this wonderful plant:

- Most bamboo reaches its full height and width in three to four months, after which it grows leafy branches outward and continues to form roots deep in the ground. The plant is fully developed after three years. Compare this to the oak tree, which can take one hundred to one hundred fifty years to reach its tallest height!

- Experts disagree on how many species of bamboo exist, but most estimate that there are at least one thousand species of bamboo in the world. Some bamboo species flower only three or four times in one hundred years.

- Bamboo contains natural substances that make it antibacterial. These substances can prevent up to 70 percent of bacteria from growing on it, making bamboo a great material to use in cooking tools.
- Speaking of cooking, many people eat cooked bamboo shoots, but watch out—the shoots are poisonous if they're not boiled before being eaten.
- Talk about a growth spurt! The record for fastest growth of a bamboo plant is 47.6 inches in just twenty-four hours.
- Bamboo plants release 30 percent more oxygen into the atmosphere than deciduous trees (trees such as oak, maple, and elm) or other plants.

Independence Celebrations Around the World

America isn't the only country that celebrates its independence with food, fun, and fireworks! Check out these other nations' dazzling displays.

India—India observes its independence day on August 15, when more than 300 years of British rule in India came to an end in 1947. To the people of India, kite-flying symbolizes freedom: Many people make kites in the colors of the national flag and fly them throughout the day.

INDIA

Cambodia—November 9 marks the day Cambodia gained its independence from France in 1953. Colorful parades and parties occur throughout the capital city, and the city's buildings and monuments are all lit up at night.

CAMBODIA

Mexico—Mexico celebrates its independence day on September 16 with a reenactment of the *Grito de Dolores* or "Cry of Dolores." Dolores was the town from which Miguel Hidalgo y Costilla launched the Mexican War of Independence, which ended in 1821.

MEXICO

Colombia—Colombians celebrate their independence from Spain on July 20, when the country formed its first representative council in 1810. Parties center around Colombian music, food, dance, and of course, the Colombian flag.

COLOMBIA

France—France's independence day, better known as "Bastille Day," is commemorated on

FRANCE

July 14, when revolutionaries stormed the Bastille fortress, kicking off the French Revolution in 1789. The day is celebrated with fireworks, parties, and parades.

Greece—Greece's independence day is honored on March 25, the same date as the beginning of the War of Greek Independence in 1821. Every year across the country schoolchildren march in their town's parade wearing traditional Greek clothes and holding the Greek flag.

GREECE

The Color Wheel

There's a lot that goes into the creation of fireworks, but getting the fireworks' colors exactly right can be especially tricky—as you already learned, specific chemicals have to be added in just the right amounts to make the fireworks burn in different hues. How well do you know your colors?

The color wheel is a helpful tool that can show us how colors are related. A basic color wheel can be made using primary and secondary colors.

Red, yellow, and blue are the three **primary colors**. We call them primary because they cannot be made by mixing two other colors together.

Green, orange, and violet are the three **secondary colors**. Each of these colors is a mixture of two primary colors.

Check out the position of the colors on the wheel. Each secondary color is placed between the primary colors we use to make it.

By mixing together red and yellow, we get orange.

By mixing together yellow and blue, we get green.

By mixing together blue and red, we get violet.

Being an expert on something means you can get an awesome score on a quiz on that subject! Take this

HISTORY OF FIREWORKS QUIZ

to see how much you've learned.

1. The first fireworks were made from the stalk of which plant?

   a. buttercup   b. bamboo   c. corn

2. What ingredient did Chinese alchemists create that made fireworks give off a flash of light?

   a. gunpowder   b. ketchup   c. rubber

3. Which famous explorer may have brought gunpowder to Europe in the thirteenth century?

   a. Hernán Cortés   b. Marco Polo   c. Ferdinand Magellan

4. Fireworks experts were known as "fire masters," but what were their assistants called?

   a. Blue Men   b. Martians   c. Green Men

5. What did the assistants of the "fire masters" wear on their heads for protection?

   a. caps made of leaves   b. helmets   c. wool hats

6. Ingredients such as barium, lithium, and copper have what effect on fireworks?

   a. change their color   b. make them louder   c. make them fly higher

7. John Adams wanted to use fireworks to celebrate which new holiday?

   a. Independence Day   b. Thanksgiving   c. Presidents' Day

8. Today people who design and set off fireworks shows are known by what title?

   a. doctors   b. pyrotechnicians   c. attorneys

9. On India's Independence Day, how do most people celebrate?

   a. making confetti   b. painting eggs   c. flying kites

Answers: 1. b 2. a 3. b 4. c 5. a 6. a 7. a 8. b 9. c